Rossini

THE GREAT COMPOSERS

ROSSINI

by
JAMES HARDING

THOMAS Y. CROWELL COMPANY
New York

To the memory of
Sir Thomas Beecham and Francis Toye,
Rossinians par excellence

Contents

Illustrations

Music Examples

I

'*Little Adonis*'

Rossini loved a joke. This was clear from the very beginning, since he chose to make his first appearance in life on the 29th February 1792. Strictly speaking, as a Leap Year baby, he was only entitled to celebrate a birthday every four years. So, although he lived to be seventy-six, he had only been able to celebrate eighteen 'calendar' birthdays in the course of his long life! In 1968, the year of his centenary, he would have reached the grand old age of forty-eight. It is just the sort of situation he would have turned into an opera, full of comic misunderstandings and involved situations.

The Rossini family had once been aristocratic. They had a coat of arms to prove it, showing a nightingale on a rose. Only after the family had long since become impoverished was the nightingale justified, and then it was through the achievements of its most famous member, rather than through the work of the ambassador who graced its ranks in the early days of prosperity. The Rossini wealth and reputation had dwindled long before the end of the eighteenth century. One of the last people to bear the name was Giuseppe Rossini. He lived in the fishing port of Pesaro, a small town nestling on the shore of the blue Adriatic. The houses were tall and over-hung narrow cobbled streets. Safely distant from the raucous bustle of the fish market stood the town's only distinguished piece of architecture, the fifteenth-century ducal palace. Farther up the coast was the old city of Rimini, more dignified perhaps than Pesaro and more beautiful, but certainly no livelier than the noisy, exuberant place of Rossini's birth.

Rossini's father was what we would call a 'character'. He owed his nick-name, *il Vivazza*, to a personality as vivacious as it was fiery. Everyone in Pesaro knew Vivazza. If you did not meet him socially you could be sure of coming across him in at least one of his official functions, since this versatile man earned his living as a musician in the local theatre band, as Town Crier, and as Inspector of Slaughterhouses. Each of these different jobs he carried out with an endearing flourish.

One day he met a nineteen-year-old dressmaker called Anna Guidarini. With her glossy black hair and pert features she was a renowned local beauty and had a train of admirers. Vivazza adored her, he fell in love with her at once, and when Anna was expecting a child they decided to marry.

On 29th February 1792 a boy was born. They christened him Gioacchino and spoiled him outrageously. He inherited the dark-eyed good looks of his mother, and with them a charm that few grown-ups could resist. So handsome was he that they called him 'little Adonis'. From his father came the boundless vivacity that was constantly leading him into scrapes. His fondness for practical jokes was unquenchable.

It is said that he raided sacristies and drank the Communion wine. Another well-known incident occurred when the precocious boy fell in love at the age of ten. He met his girl-friend secretly in a church to exchange kisses and pledges of undying affection. A furious priest overheard them and chased the irreverent pair from the holy place, beating them with the cords of his robe. But no one could be angry for long with little Adonis, and his winning manner quickly restored him to favour, however disgraceful his escapades had been.

Lazy, wayward and trading unscrupulously on his charm, the boy sometimes reduced even his easy-going parents to despair. It was difficult enough for them to bring him up in settled surroundings. Vivazza had an unfortunate habit of expressing his political opinions with more vigour than discretion and he lost his job. During the political struggles of 1796 he was sent to prison for declaring himself on the side of the French and in favour of the republican government.

Throughout the years of Rossini's boyhood his parents were forced to lead a vagabond life. Vivazza played in the pit of theatres and took what jobs he could to keep body and soul together. Anna Rossini performed in operas, and, though she had had no training, sang by ear very well. 'In fact,' said Rossini later, 'she was ignorant of music but she had a wonderful memory . . . and that was how she easily learned the roles given to her. Her naturally expressive voice was lovely and full of grace—sweet, like her appearance.'

While the Rossinis travelled the country for work their mischievous son was boarded out in Pesaro. Sent as a punishment to pump the bellows of a smithy, he found that listening to the blows on the anvil improved his sense of rhythm. His naughtiness persisted. Anna Rossini was driven to tears by her son's unruliness. But if there was one person whom 'little Adonis' loved

Above: the composer's parents, Anna and Giuseppe Rossini
Left: Rossini's birth-place, Pesaro

Above left: a portrait of
Rossini by Marzocchi
Above right: a drawing by
Sir Thomas Lawrence
Left: Isabella Colbran,
Rossini's first wife, in
operatic costume

and respected it was his mother. Touched by her distress, he applied himself seriously to music lessons. Even here an element of comedy prevailed.
His piano teacher was a man who, possessed of a many-sidedness compar-
able to Vivazza's, dabbled with equal gusto in music and the wine trade.
This eccentric figure taught his pupils to play scales by using only the
thumb and first finger. He had no permanent home and slept at night in
the streets. This was the cause of his tendency to doze off during lessons,
and it was a habit that saved Rossini a lot of work. When the drowsy
teacher woke up from one of his prolonged naps the boy would tell him, all
blandness and sincerity, that he had already played his piece.

Better teachers followed. In 1805, when the family at last came to rest
in Bologna, Rossini was accepted as a student at the famous Liceo Musicale.
He proved to have a good voice and sang frequently in churches and
theatres where he served as chorus-master and earned a welcome addition to
the family income. His father taught him to play the horn and he quickly
mastered the cello, viola and cembalo. It was not long before he realized
that his true ambition was to compose. At twelve he produced six string
sonatas, written and copied out in the space of three days. His love for
Haydn and Mozart, whose work he studied with eagerness, earned him the
nickname of *il Tedeschino*, 'the little German'. Another of his idols was the
Italian composer Cimarosa, whose operas were to influence his own music.

Rossini was easily bored by the work his teacher gave him. He was de-
pressed by the lessons in musical theory given him by a dry-as-dust teacher
who insisted on strict observance of the rules of composition. 'Why do I
have to keep to the rules?' he complained. 'Because that's the way things
are done,' he was firmly told. With a sigh he went back to his furtive study
of Haydn and Mozart—furtive, because in those days Bologna, a famous
musical capital, did not easily grant the seal of respectability to such composers. Yet from their pages Rossini learned far more than from his lessons.
His impatience with his teachers is understandable. When you have natural
gifts that enable you to write down the piano score of a complete opera from
memory after only one hearing, you can be forgiven for chafing at conven-
tional methods.

When he was eighteen Rossini asked his teacher what else remained for
him to study.

Plainchant and fugue, he was told. How long would all that take?
Another two years, came the answer. Rossini exploded with frustration. He
had a living to earn! He had already turned out a quantity of chamber
music, a mass, a symphony, and a two-act opera written when he was four-

teen. He was anxious to spread his wings because, intuitively, he knew that he had absorbed all the academic grounding his genius needed. There was also the pressing need to earn money for the family, an urge that throughout his career was to push him into a non-stop round of composing. So with his scores in his pocket he stepped forth from the Liceo Musicale and bounced confidently into the world outside.

Almost immediately a bit of luck came his way. Four years previously, while playing in a theatre orchestra, he had burst into loud laughter at the *prima donna*'s grotesque failure to hit a high note. The furious singer instructed her impresario to rebuke the impudent youngster. This the impresario had done, but, as usual in such cases, he was easily pacified by Rossini's engaging charm. Once his anger had cooled he could not help noticing the boy's obvious talent and ambition. He decided to keep an eye on him. Just about the time Rossini bade farewell to the Liceo, the impresario had trouble on his hands in Venice. The composer of a one-act opera had failed to supply the music. Anxious not to miss his opening date, the impresario thought of Rossini. Would he step into the breach? He would indeed. He left post-haste for the city of lagoons and, more important still, of keen opera audiences.

Within a few days he had written *la Cambiale di matrimonio*, or 'Marriage by Promissory Note'. For the first time he saw his name on a theatre bill and moved among the smell of oranges and grease-paint as if by right. It was also his first experience as the target of temperamental singers who are never satisfied with the music written for them and who complain bitterly that the composer has not given them the chance to show off their flashy talents. The atmosphere of rehearsals was turbulent and the stormy quarrels reduced Rossini to tears. Luckily his opera was a success. The audience warmly applauded the emergence of a new and striking talent. The farcical plot which it prefaces tells of an unromantic merchant called Slook, who tries to run his courtship and marriage on approved commercial lines. The libretto is not uproariously funny, but Rossini made it seem better than it was with music that even a hundred-and-fifty years later froths with gaiety. The fact that it was written by a youth still in his 'teens makes it something of a miracle.

La Cambiale brought Rossini 200 *lire*, or a sum equal to roughly fifty pounds (one hundred and forty dollars) in modern currency. 'I've never had so much money in my hands before!' he exclaimed triumphantly. He promptly sent it off to his beloved mother. On the envelope he wrote her address:

'Little Adonis'

To Signora Rossini,
mother of the famous *maestro* Gioacchino Rossini,
via Maggiore 240,
Bologna.

The Rossini coat of arms

II

Silken Ladders and Italian Girls

Rossini now found himself plunged into a life in which there was enough colourful incident and vivid atmosphere to satisfy even his restless taste for variety. The Italian operatic world then was, as now, a rumbustious and clamorous one. Triumph announced itself in garish tints. Failure was depicted in the blackest shades. Everyday existence was a series of flamboyant crises which did not end when the curtain fell and which continued to seethe still more violently in the wings. Singers travelled from town to town and spent long hours bumping along dusty roads in weather-beaten carriages.

Most Italian towns with any civic pride held opera seasons at their local theatre. One of the richer citizens usually made himself responsible for assembling a troupe of singers. Then he would search out a poet to write a libretto and find a composer to provide the notes. The business manager, we are told, was often some shady lawyer who contrived to enrich himself on the side. For weeks ahead the town would bubble with scandal about the *prima donna*'s love affairs and backstage intrigues. In the absence of any other entertainment the opera was anticipated with intense eagerness. Audiences' reactions were ruthless and voluble. They were as likely to bellow 'Bravo, maestro,' as they were to damn the luckless performers with jeers and cat-calls.

This was the world Rossini knew for the next twenty or so years. Like his parents before him he ranged the country as a wandering minstrel. Often he wrote as many as four operas in twelve months to keep up with public demand. His reputation grew. On arriving in a town he would be greeted by the local notabilities and fêted at receptions. His good looks and his wit soon made him a hero with the ladies. He liked women. They liked him. He was not only clever, they found, but anxious to please them as well, and he flattered his way to many a conquest. His enjoyment of social life gave little time for writing music. This did not matter since he composed astonishingly quickly and never had to wait for inspiration. He composed anywhere at any time, preferably surrounded by a group of chattering friends and hangers-on. The legends began to accumulate around him. He once, it was said, wrote an overture in the time it took to boil a dish of rice. His favourite place for composition was in bed. The story goes that when he accidentally dropped the sheets of an aria on to the floor, he was too lazy to get out and pick them up. So he calmly wrote another to take its place.

When the people of a town commissioned him to write an opera, he would first make a brief visit to their theatre and meet the troupe who had been engaged. A few chords on the piano, a few scales from the singers, were enough to give him an idea of the company's abilities. Then he would be off on his social rounds, scribbling the required music in between parties and usually leaving the overture to be written on the night before the first performance. His wonderful gift rarely let him down. Added to which he was a practical man of the theatre who had learned his craft in the best possible way, by tough and often humiliating experience. It is a characteristic of genius to be able to do things much more quickly and correctly than ordinary men. Like Mozart, Rossini had a lightning intuition and a speed of assimilation which carried him at a remarkable rate through the massive drudgery of writing an opera. The labour of noting down page after page of full orchestral score is enough to daunt any man, let alone the constant worry of bearing in mind the needs of different types of voice and the demands of stage technique.

When the curtain fell, when the candlelight was snuffed out and the exhausted singers had taken off their paint, Rossini and his colleagues bowled away through the night to their next engagement. Life was exacting and conditions were hard. He did not care. He had his youth and his popularity. If disaster struck, the next turn in the road would as likely bring success. And always, even in the midst of a party or a flirtation, his musical subconscious was absorbing ideas and impressions. It was perhaps on one of these tours that he came across the folk tune he uses so memorably in *il Barbiere di Siviglia*:

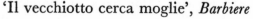

'Il vecchiotto cerca moglie', *Barbiere*

It would have amused Rossini had he known that one day scholars would examine his music and puzzle over its frequent discrepancies. His operas were, like Shakespeare's plays, written to entertain an audience of decided views and tastes. The public was his master and he must please it to live. Scenes were adapted or dropped, arias replaced and songs adjusted, in the light of audience reaction. To save time, Rossini often used an aria which had been popular in other towns. This explains why the same tunes occasionally occur in operas which are completely different from each other and why whole overtures often do duty several times over. Rossini had no exalted ideas about his art. He was the servant of his public. 'Give me a laundry list and I'll set it to music,' he joked. Music was to be enjoyed with as much relish as good food and pretty women. It was this healthy attitude which in the past led the puritanical English to dismiss Rossini as trivial. They were wrong.

In the spring of 1812 Rossini came back to Venice, the scene of his first success, with a new work ready for production. It was called *la Scala di seta*, or 'The Silken Ladder', another farcical opera. Alas, this time the critical Venetians were not so indulgent towards him. The overture is often played today and is the first in which he fully develops his characteristic treatment of the form.

Later that year in Milan Rossini was to make up for this minor setback with an opera which won him new favour. *La Pietra del paragone* ('The

Touchstone') is the story of a rich Count who pretends to have lost all his money so as to test the sincerity of three ladies who claim to be in love with him. A recent Glyndebourne revival has shown us why the opera so delighted people over a century-and-a-half ago. The overture, which was also used for *Tancredi* a few years later, has a famous allegro passage. With its springy rhythm and jaunty octave leaps, it gives a splendid foretaste of the vitality that runs all the way through *la Pietra*:

Overture, *la Pietra del paragone*

The vast auditorium of La Scala, all white, red and gold, was filled with applause for the new maestro. A run of fifty performances straight off made Rossini the talk of the town. He was granted the privilege of exemption from military service. It was an honour he appreciated quite as much as the fame and fortune that had come to him. He was franker than most when he cheerfully admitted to cowardice and an utter lack of soldierly qualities. In fact, he pointed out with a smile, his exemption was a distinct advantage to the army.

Rossini enjoyed his triumph to the full. Impresarios crowded round to ask him for more operas. Singers begged him to use his influence on their behalf. Restaurant proprietors welcomed him gladly, knowing that he would order the best and most expensive dishes on the menu. Within eleven days he had written a one-act comic opera entitled *l'Occasione fa il ladro*, or 'Opportunity makes the thief'. As if to demonstrate that the theatre is a fickle mistress, the piece had only five performances. Its failure was undeserved, for there are a number of good things are to be found in it.

Equally unsuccessful was *il Signor Bruschino*. Only the overture now survives. It is unusual in that the second violins are instructed to tap out the rhythm in several passages with their bows. This novel effect failed to amuse the public. Years later the Parisian composer Offenbach produced *il Signor Bruschino* at his own theatre and invited Rossini to attend. He declined. It was enough for him to have encouraged Offenbach, he wryly observed, without going to the extreme of acting as his accomplice.

Early next year the wheel of fortune turned again and Rossini was the idol of Venetian audiences. The occasion was *Tancredi*, his first venture into *opera seria* as distinct from the comic operas he had been writing until then. The new work, an account of the adventures of the Norman knight Tancred during the Saracen wars, caught the imagination of Venice. One aria in particular, 'Di tanti palpiti', was a tremendous 'hit'. Everyone went about humming it. Testy judges, it was said, even had to rebuke members of the public for whistling the tune in court. This aria, typically, was written in haste at the last minute:

Aria, 'Di tanti palpiti', *Tancredi*

Silken Ladders and Italian Girls

The melody is deceptively simple. Where a lesser composer would have fallen into the trap of writing mere barrel-organ music, Rossini, with the neatest of touches, distils a beautifully plaintive quality. The fame of *Tancredi* spread gradually beyond Venice. Other towns took up the chivalrous tale and thrilled to its spectacle of gallantry. The whole of Europe now sang Rossini's tunes.

Silken Ladders and Italian Girls

His star had never shone more brightly. His dark eyes twinkling with mischief, his features lit with a captivating smile, he was sought after by the most fashionable society in Venice. He was a hearty performer at the dinner table and soon established a reputation as a lover of good food. His appetite for Bologna hams, Parmesan cheeses and richly spiced sausages was unquenchable. When the inhabitants of Pesaro proposed to build a statue to their most famous son, he remarked that he'd have preferred a bunch of *mortadella* sausages instead.

Somehow or other he found time to write another opera. It took him, so they say, just over three weeks. A few months after *Tancredi* he again delighted Venice with *l'Italiana in Algeri*. The adventures of the Italian girl in Algiers, which can now be seen on the stage at Sadler's Wells, involve her attempts to save her lover from the clutches of the Bey—only to find herself clapped into the latter's harem. There she uses her wily feminine charms to outwit the absurd old Bey and to rescue the man she loves. The music ripples along in a glittering stream of tireless comic invention. While the fun never stops, there are none the less moments of delicate feeling. One such is the wistful cavatina in which Lindoro, the Italian girl's lover, bewails the torment of longing for a beautiful lady who is far away. The melody is first heard as a horn *obbligato*.

Both in style and treatment, this opera has a strong flavour of the Mozart whom Rossini adored—the Mozart of *il Seraglio* and *Die Zauberflöte*.

Few composers have known success so early and so abundantly as Rossini. At the age of twenty-one he was rich, famous and admired. The adulation he received did not turn his head, and one of his most endearing qualities was a complete lack of vanity. He never boasted about his music and gently deflected excessive compliments with some witty phrase. Asked which of his own works he preferred, he once replied: 'I prefer... Cimarosa's *il Matrimonio segreto*.' He was generous in recognizing other men's talent. When he heard Bellini's first opera he gracefully congratulated him: 'Young man! you are beginning your career at a point where many "great" ones end theirs.'

As he wandered through the streets of Venice, acknowledging the respectful bow of a music-loving gondolier or the inviting flash of a pair of dark eyes, he could be forgiven for thinking that life would always favour him. Precocious though he was, he had not yet fully realized that fate was often unbearably capricious, and that in the theatre the rewards of success are so frequently soured by the failures that accompany them. His sunny optimism took no account of the malice he was to incur from envious rivals, nor did he foresee the heavy price he was to pay at a later date in shattered nerves and ruined health. For the moment, everything looked perfect. And, anyway, at his age he would have been a fool to worry about the future.

III

Interlude: Rossini and the Overture

By the time he reached his early twenties, Rossini's style was already mature. At this point it would be interesting to look at some of his characteristics as a composer. His overtures, for example, are instantly recognizable. The conductor who wants to get his programme off to a brilliant start knows that a good way of doing it is to open with any one of a dozen Rossini overtures. It often happens that some of these overtures are extremely famous, while the operas to which they belong are rarely heard. One reason is that in the early part of last century it was not by any means a firm rule that an overture should contain melodies which occur in the opera itself. In fact, the overture to *il Barbiere di Siviglia* had already been used for *Aureliano in Palmira* and *Elisabetta, regina d'Inghilterra*. (It is true, however, that the concluding theme of this overture emerges very effectively in the finale to Act I of the last-named opera.) Another reason is that in the noisy Italian theatres of the day the overtures was regarded as a useful means of reminding people that the entertainment was about to start. Rossini was content to produce self-contained pieces of music which are always a pleasure to hear for the sake of their liveliness and good humour.

The overtures usually open with a chord or a passage loud enough to still a chattering audience, yet interesting enough to arouse expectation. Such is the case with the overture to *la Cenerentola* ('Cinderella') which also served for *il Turco in Italia*. In the case of *la Gazza ladra* ('The Thieving Magpie'), Rossini astonished his audience by starting with two sudden drum rolls—a very novel idea for the time—as an introduction to one of the cockiest and most self-confident marches ever written.

Interlude: *Rossini and the Overture*

Overture, *la Gazza ladra*

Once the audience's attention is well and truly captured, Rossini goes on to charm us with one of those tunes guaranteed to set everyone's foot tapping. Perhaps the most famous is the melody which comes tripping in after the long and majestic introduction to *il Barbiere*. Just as typical is the tune quoted from *la Pietra del paragone* (see pages 23–24).

From then onwards the pace becomes faster and the volume louder. There is little 'development' in the strict sense, but sudden key changes and unexpected variation of the instrumental groupings whip up the frenzy in

30

a steady *crescendo* until the orchestra triumpantly reaches the final double-*forte* chord and the curtain rises. Rossini often used the device of gradually loudening the music so that excitement reaches fever pitch in the end. It is one of his most obvious tricks and it earned him the not very friendly nick-name of 'Signor Crescendo' or 'Signor Vacarmini' (Franco-Italian for 'Mister Noisy'). It must be admitted that he takes a boyish delight in big drums and the instruments of percussion generally. He also adopts the *crescendo* for vocal purposes. One of his most effective uses of it comes in the great aria where Don Basilio, with increasing vivacity, describes how a small rumour can pass from mouth to mouth until it grows into a monstrous slander. Nearly always Rossini employs the technique in the right place to emphasize drama or emotion.

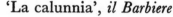

'La calunnia', *il Barbiere*

He was, of course, much more than a specialist in *crescendo*. His mastery of orchestration told him, with unerring instinct, which instrument could best be used for certain passages. In particular he wrote beautifully for the wind players. We take these passages for granted nowadays, but in Rossini's time such treatment was an innovation. The following bars from the over-ture to *la Gazza ladra* give an excellent opportunity to the cool, silvery tones of the oboe. Then the flute takes over in unison with strings, and the clarinet and bassoon join in at the final flourish:

Olympe Pélissier, Rossini's second wife   Rossini, *c.* 1860

The composer's music room at the Academy of Music, Bologna

Rossini's funeral cortège, Paris, 1868

Rossini's reburial at Santa Croce, Florence, 1887

Interlude: Rossini and the Overture

Oboe solo, *la Gazza ladra*

Throughout the overtures and the operas that follow them there are in-
numerable solo or concerted passages, all flecked with genius, all lending
beauty to the themes and offering individual players a chance to shine.

With the overture to *Guillaume Tell*, his last opera, Rossini took great
pains. For the first time in his career he wrote an overture which is recog-
nizably linked to the story and which mirrors important events in it. The
result is an ingenious tone poem in miniature. A tranquil introduction pic-
tures dawn rising over the Swiss mountains. This is followed by scurrying
violins which depict a storm on Lake Lucerne and remind us that Rossini
was a particularly accomplished writer of 'storm music'. The next section
evokes a charming pastoral scene with the aid of the cor anglais, an instrument which Rossini was among the earliest to use in such a distinctive way:

Interlude: Rossini and the Overture

Cor anglais and flute solo, *Guillaume Tell*

Interlude: Rossini and the Overture

The overture ends with the famous 'quick march' which was originally intended to be sung at the end of the second act. Unfortunately, it has become so popular and has been ground out over and over again by so many
bad brass bands that people have heard it too often really to appreciate its
originality. Yet the romantic feeling of the story is attractively conveyed,
and the martial swagger of the patriots is expressed with great force.

IV

Enter the Barber

Achill wind blew and snow lay on the needle spires of Milan cathedral as Rossini's coach trundled into the city one bleak winter's day in 1813. It was a poor omen for the two operas he was to present at La Scala, where an earlier audience had acclaimed *la Pietra del paragone*. The first of these operas was chosen to open the winter Carnival season. It had a poor reception and some of the spectators even left before the performance was over. Even worse, the singer who took the leading role decorated Rossini's music with all sorts of florid extemporizations, just to show how clever he was and to win the cheers of the gallery. This sort of exhibitionism naturally infuriated Rossini. He was constantly fighting battles with vain performers who regarded his music as an excuse for their own showmanship. The great singer, Adelina Patti, who once took similar liberties with another of Rossini's arias, was icily told: 'How charming! Pray tell me, who wrote it?'

The second opera which fared badly at Milan was *il Turco in Italia*. People thought it was too close to *l'Italiana*, and the Milanese suspected they were being fobbed off with an imitation. It was all very well, they argued, to get away with it in Venice, but Milan was a different place altogether. Local pride was hurt.

Rossini shrugged his shoulders and went back to try his luck again in Venice. There he failed once more. The Venetians were unimpressed by the 'serious' opera he put before them. Their judgement has been proved correct by the passage of time, for *Sigismondo*, as it was called, soon faded into oblivion. There were, however, several good pieces to be salvaged from it by the thrifty Rossini, and among them was the *crescendo* passage (pages 31–2) which he used in *il Barbiere*.

Things seemed to have come to a dead end for the moment, so Rossini packed his bags for Bologna and licked his wounds throughout the spring of 1815 in the company of his admired, and admiring, parents. While he was there a commission reached him from the proprietor of the San Carlo opera-house at Naples. This rough and ready man, whose name was Domenico Barbaja, ran a vast business network of which his operatic ventures were only a part. Barbaja was illiterate. He was totally uneducated. His first job consisted of washing dishes in a café. Then he invented a new type of coffee-cream which he christened *Barbajata* and sold in great quantities. With the money he made he set up as a supplier of goods to the army and grew still richer. The step that brought him a huge fortune was to take over the gambling rooms attached to La Scala in Milan. Not long afterwards he was wealthy enough to buy La Scala itself! His superb flair for business enabled him later to set up in Naples and acquire the San Carlo opera-house as well. When the San Carlo was accidentally destroyed by fire, Barbaja, who knew nothing about architecture, was such a brilliant organizer that he had the whole magnificent structure rebuilt in less than a year.

Rossini got on well with Barbaja. He appreciated the self-made impresario's earthy wit and shrewd realism. Although Barbaja only paid a small monthly salary of about thirty-five pounds (one hundred dollars) in return for writing operas and doing odd jobs about the theatre, Rossini was allowed a share of the large sums taken at Barbaja's gaming table. He had free board and lodging at his employer's house into the bargain. This was a useful arrangement, as Rossini shared the plump impresario's fondness for good food.

As time went on Rossini became more and more interested in Barbaja's companion, a singer called Isabella Colbran. Her charms, in Rossini's opinion, added greatly to the beauty of the Bay of Naples, and her temperament was as fiery as the Mount Vesuvius which lay beyond. You could easily guess her Spanish origin from her coal-black hair and smouldering eyes. She was then just over thirty years old and at the height of her powers. Her singing was passionate, and the expressiveness of her acting thrilled Neapolitan audiences.

'You are the only person in the world to understand singing!' exclaimed la Colbran delightedly when Rossini unveiled the opera he had written for her as the first of his Naples commissions. One may rightly conclude that it is as well that Rossini understood singing, for his librettist certainly did not understand English history. The plot of *Elisabetta, regina d'Inghilterra*, is an unintentionally hilarious travesty of the love affairs of Queen Elizabeth I and the Earl of Leicester. However, as a recent revival has shown, this curious opera stands up well in performance. With Colbran in the cast was the famous Manuel Garcia, father of those other distinguished singers Maria Malibran and Pauline Viardot. The Neapolitans took them, and Rossini, to their hearts, and the composer once again basked in the favour that had temporarily deserted him.

Apart from the overture and other passages which Rossini later incorporated into *il Barbiere, Elisabetta* is not very well known. It is, though, worth mentioning, because in it, for the first time, he took the trouble to write out in full the ornamentation of the vocal line. Determined to frustrate the singers who embellished his music with their own flamboyant and unsuitable 'embroidery', he made sure that in future they would sing what he had written. Another technical innovation was the orchestral accompaniment he wrote for the recitatives. Up to then the accompaniment had been left to a solo instrument. Recitative is a useful device by which singers declaim the dialogue and pass on information necessary to the plot which cannot all be conveyed in the arias. By providing an orchestral accompaniment, Rossini added to the dramatic power of the music and gave it a smoother flow.

With the ovations of the Neapolitans ringing in his ears Rossini made his way to Rome. Pleased with the good value his employee had given him, Barbaja allowed Rossini to write an opera for the capital, where several of his earlier works had been applauded and had already won him a reputation. While rehearsals for his new opera were in progress, Rossini would go every day to the barber's shop for a shave. After a few visits it emerged that the barber, who wielded his cut-throat razor with a dash, was also first clarinet in the theatre orchestra. At rehearsals, whenever he played a wrong note on his clarinet, the prudent Rossini would ever afterwards take the trouble to be excessively polite in correcting him!

The Roman début turned out a failure, and those who had liked his work until now confessed to being disappointed. In his usual letter home to his mother, Rossini wrote no words but drew a large *fiasco*, a bottle in which Chianti wine is kept. It was first applied to bottles which had been distorted in the making, hence its meaning of 'failure'. There was no need for further explanation to Signora Rossini.

Her son did not mope for long. He had already signed a contract to write the opera which became *il Barbiere di Siviglia*. The original stage comedy, *le Barbier de Séville*, was the work of the French dramatist Beaumarchais, and several composers had set it before Rossini. His was the version destined to become one of the most famous and popular of all comic operas. The piece was written and rehearsed in greater haste and confusion than was usual even with Rossini. At one point he contrived to lose the overture he originally composed and had to substitute the one written for *Elisa-*

betta. Such economy is understandable when we realize that the 600 pages of his masterpiece were dashed off at staggering speed in about a fortnight —the time, it has been estimated, that a quick writer would need merely to copy them out!

The play itself is, of course, a classic, and would not have needed Rossini's music to survive. There was nothing very original in the basic materials Beaumarchais used. Many dramatists before him had relied on the stock situation of a silly old guardian whose pretty ward is filched from him by a young lover. Beaumarchais's great achievement was to immortalize an old theme with unforgettable characterization and witty dialogue. The people in *le Barbier de Séville* are as alive today as they were nearly two hundred years ago, and with tremendous vitality: the pompous Bartolo, the mischievous Rosina, her dashing lover, Count Almaviva, and the greedy Basilio.

Around and about them darts the impudent barber, Figaro, who engineers the abduction of Rosina. Here is the lively aria in which he tells what a busy life he leads:

Aria, 'Largo al factotum', *il Barbiere*

Enter the Barber

There is a great deal of Rossini himself in Figaro. Never at a loss for a smart reply, always on top of the situation and perpetually amused at his own resourcefulness, he usually managed to fall on his feet. When Figaro says: 'I am quick to laugh at everything for fear of being obliged to weep,' he sums up rather neatly what might have been Rossini's own philosophy.

From the moment the overture begins the opera bustles along at a cracking pace. There is tremendous variety in it. At one moment there is the polished virtuosity of Rosina as she sings of hearing her lover's voice a little while ago:

Aria, 'Una voce poco fa', *il Barbiere*

Enter the Barber

At another, there is sly humour as Rossini so cleverly portrays the bumbling self-importance of Dr. Bartolo. For a learned man, a doctor like myself, he tells Rosina, you must offer better excuses for your naughtiness (see page 44).

The *Barbiere* is so packed with lovely things that the only way to do them full justice is to play the whole score over and over again, and to listen to it as much as you can. You will then see why Rossini's sense of fun has charmed many generations of opera-goers and why his work is hailed as a classic.

Aria, 'A un dottor della mia sorte', *il Barbiere*

Strangely, the opera was not immediately successful. The first night was chaotic. One of the leading singers tripped up and had to sing while trying to stop his nose bleeding. The audience jeered and whistled at Rossini who led the orchestra from the cembalo, as was usual in those days. Then a cat wandered on to the stage during the finale. On the second night Rossini prudently stayed at home in bed. After this unfortunate start, though, the *Barbiere* soon became popular throughout the world.

For this great work Rossini was paid the equivalent of roughly five hundred pounds, or fourteen hundred dollars. The sum was a large one for the period, but the principal singers received nearly three times as much. He was also given a nut-brown suit with gilt buttons. It was a gift from his impresario, who, as Rossini said later, was anxious that he should look 'decently dressed in the orchestra pit'. He was particularly pleased with the handsome buttons.

V

Cinderella and Marriage

Proudly displaying his nut-brown suit with its gilt buttons, Rossini came back to Naples to carry on with his work for Barbaja. He found the macaroni there as succulent as ever. La Colbran looked just as beautiful, perhaps even more so after his absence. The opera he wrote for her on his return was not a success. With his next work it was a different story, and in it la Colbran scored a triumph which was to last for many years.

Otello was Rossini's nineteenth opera. Though very popular in its time it has long since been overshadowed by Verdi's opera on the same subject. English people familiar with Shakespeare's tragedy find the libretto Rossini used quite absurd. There is some lovely music in it, but it is hampered by the silly plot.

Far more to everyone's taste today is Rossini's opera about Cinderella, *la Cenerentola*. It was done in Rome for the Christmas of 1816. He set the libretto piecemeal as it was delivered to him, and in about three weeks he completed a work that is sometimes considered to be the equal of the *Bar-biere*.

Yet *Cenerentola* is by no means all buffoonery. Ragged Cinderella sits by the fire and muses, with sweet melancholy, on the King who lived long ago and chose a humble girl of the people for his bride:

Aria, 'Una volta c'era un re', *la Cenerentola*

46

so - lo, che a star so - lo s'an-no - jò; cer - ça, cer - ca, ri - tro -

- vò: ma il vo-lean spo - sa - re_ in tre. Co - sa

fa? sprez-za il fa - sto e_ la bel - tà, e al - la fin scel-se per

sè l'in-no - cen - za, l'in-no-cen - za, l'in - no - cen - za e_ la bon -

-tà la la la la li li li li la la la la.

The fairy story ends, like traditional pantomime, with a magnificent scene where the heroine takes her throne. Accompanied by one of those blithe and stirring choruses Rossini produced with such joyous inspiration, she sings a final aria resplendent with breath-taking vocal fireworks. (Rossini 'lifted' it, in fact, from his own *Barbiere*!)

La Cenerentola, like so many of Rossini's operas, is very difficult to sing. It demands performers of great skill and experience. That is one reason why, until it was revived by Sadler's Wells, it has not very often been heard in modern times.

Over the next few years Rossini kept his headquarters at Naples, with occasional ventures to Rome, Venice and Milan. After *la Cenerentola* he wrote no more genuinely 'Italian' comic operas. Instead, between 1817 and 1822, he composed more than half a dozen serious works intended to display the talents of Isabella Colbran. It was probably due to her influence that he deserted the field of comic opera, where he was an undisputed master, and concentrated on the melodramatic subjects which gave her the opportunity she wanted to exploit her gift for tragedy.

The plots Rossini set to music came from a wild and unlikely variety of sources. There was one that thrilled audiences no end with an exciting climax where Colbran, as a patriotic Greek girl, died nobly among the ruins of Corinth. When Rossini settled in France he revised it under the title of *le Siège de Corinthe*. Another plot was taken from Sir Walter Scott's poem, 'The Lady of the Lake', which became *la Donna del lago*. The fierce Scottish chieftain, Roderick Dhu, was turned into Roderigo di Dhu, and the young lover, Malcolm Graeme, was played, like a pantomime 'principal boy', by a woman. The romantic flavour of Scott's work had a fascination for Italian opera composers which often proved fatal.

An opera which Rossini gave towards the end of this period is remembered today chiefly for the unusual circumstances under which he wrote it. With him in Rome at the time was the violinist Niccolò Paganini. His wonderful playing, the like of which had never been heard before, gave rise to the belief that Paganini was in league with the Devil. His appearance, mysterious and lantern-jawed, certainly helped the eerie legend. While Rossini was busily composing *Matilde di Shabran*, Paganini would pick up the freshly-written sheets and play them with dazzling variations. He also helped out by taking over the first performance after the conductor had fallen ill. At Carnival time he and Rossini dressed up as women and strummed guitars for alms in the street, Paganini 'thin as a door and with a face like the handle of his violin', and Rossini presenting the spectacle of his 'already ample form stuffed with bundles of straw'.

48

Cinderella and Marriage

Despite the absurdities of the operas Rossini composed during his years at Naples, we should not ignore the quantity of fine music that often lies buried in those long-forgotten pieces. Nobody who worked as hard and as constantly as Rossini could avoid producing much that was bad tangled up with much that was good. An oratorio about Moses, later converted into French as the grand opera *Moïse*, caused a great sensation. The resourceful librettist contrived to introduce a love affair into the old Biblical story, so providing an excuse for Isabella Colbran to win new applause from her admirers. Unfortunately the big moment, where the Red Sea parts and then closes to overwhelm Pharaoh's army, went badly wrong. The audience roared with laughter when the stage machinery was revealed, showing little boys operating the painted canvas 'waves'. To avoid this difficulty Rossini speedily wrote a prayer for Moses to sing:

Preghiera, *Moïse*

This had such an effect on sensitive young ladies that a Neapolitan doctor reported over forty cases of nervous collapse in a year being brought on by it! Throughout the world the famous prayer enjoyed enormous popularity. We may not collapse with emotion on hearing it these days, but we can at least appreciate its simple beauty.

Music flowed from Rossini with the spontaneity of a Schubert. 'When will you stop writing four or five operas a year?' his father asked him. 'Never, Papa!' he replied. That was during the Neapolitan years which were perhaps the happiest time of his life. On the other hand, the cares and worries of the operatic world, he once remarked, made all impresarios in Italy go bald by the age of thirty. Not the least of their problems was the nonchalant behaviour of Rossini himself. To make him write the long-delayed overture to *Otello*, Barbaja, 'the baldest and most ferocious of all impresarios', locked

Marietta Alboni as Semiramide, by Giraud

him up in a room with a plate of macaroni and the threat that he would not be released until he had completed the music down to the last note. Another desperate impresario forced him to compose an overture on the very day of a first performance by shutting him up in an attic. Four burly stagehands kept watch outside to collect each sheet as it was finished and rushed it off to the copyists.

As the end of Rossini's Neapolitan contract tying him to Barbaja came in sight, he decided at last to marry Isabella Colbran. Perhaps he wished to regularize a situation which, having existed in fact for several years, may have begun to disturb the religious scruples of the parents he loved. Perhaps he felt that by this time Barbaja's original affection for la Colbran had cooled as a result of her temperamental behaviour. She was, moreover, a very rich woman. Among her possessions were a villa in Castenaso, which is not far from Bologna, and an estate in Sicily. The dowry she brought him was worth considerably more than £70,000 or $200,000 in today's money. Rossini was thirty and she was seven years older. The difference in age was no great handicap, for they had known each other long enough to recognize and tolerate their respective failings. They were married at Castenaso in March 1822, and the bride settled upon her newly-acquired husband a generous share of her belongings.

Barbaja did not seem to object to the new arrangement. There was no bad blood between the three of them, and he continued to make business arrangements on their behalf. He took a theatre in Vienna and organized a Rossini festival there. From Bologna, where the Rossini parents, happy to see their boy settled down to marriage, bade them farewell, the couple started their journey for the capital of Austria without having had time for a honeymoon. A new phase in Rossini's career had begun.

VI

Beethoven, Babylon, London and Paris

The Viennese already knew Rossini's work. The tunes from *il Barbiere* and half a dozen other operas were familiar to all those who appreciated music. To disarm the people who objected on patriotic grounds to this noisy Italian invasion, Barbaja very cleverly persuaded the German composer Weber to write a new opera which could be played in the same bill as Rossini's *Zelmira*. Weber's contribution was the famous *Euryanthe*, and during the festival he also conducted *Der Freischütz*.

The two great composers were utterly different from every point of view. Rossini mingled happily in society, buoyed up with past success and delighting everyone with what a newspaper called his 'vivacious talk'. Poor Weber, shy and in bad health, recoiled from the exuberance of his Italian rival and could not help envying him his popularity. He bitterly attacked Rossini in his writings and never lost an opportunity to belittle him. Rossini bore him no ill will.

A few years later an incident occurred which does credit to them both. They met in Paris, where Weber was on his way to produce *Oberon* in London. He was obviously very ill, on the point of death and 'a heart-rending sight'. He offered faltering apologies for his earlier attacks. Rossini gracefully replied that, not understanding German, he had failed to read them. The only words of German he knew, he added, were 'Ich bin zufrieden' ('I am well pleased'). And he warmly embraced the ailing Weber.

An equally celebrated event was the visit Rossini paid to Beethoven while in Vienna. He felt deeply moved as he went up the stairs that led to Beethoven's shabby lodging. At the top he found a dirty hovel, incredibly untidy, with a holed ceiling that must have let in torrents of rain. He was struck by the sadness of Beethoven's features and by his eyes, which, though small and buried like caverns beneath heavy brows, seemed to look right through him. Beethoven, though only fifty-one, had but five more years to

53

live. He was nearly stone-deaf, his poverty was extreme, and illness had undermined his health.

'Ah! Rossini. You're the one who wrote the *Barbiere di Siviglia*?' he grunted, raising his tousled head from a proof he had been correcting. Speaking in fair Italian, he went on: 'I congratulate you. It's an excellent comic opera. I've read it with pleasure and enjoyed it. It will be played for as long as Italian opera exists. Never try to write anything else but comic opera. To want to succeed in another style would harm your personality.'

Beethoven's wise advice came too late, for, as we know, Rossini had already written many serious operas for Isabella Colbran instead of the light works at which he excelled. The historic interview came to an end with Beethoven praising the Italian genius for comic opera. In return, Rossini, who knew Beethoven's quartets and some of his piano pieces, and had just been overwhelmed at his first hearing of the 'Eroica' Symphony in Vienna, told Beethoven's how much he admired his music, how grateful he felt at having been able to meet him. 'O, what an unhappy man am I!' groaned Beethoven.

'Remember,' was his last remark, 'write many more like *Barbiere*.' Rossini went down the stairs with tears in his eyes. He felt uneasy at the contrast between his own great luck and the depths of wretchedness in which Beethoven lived. When he tried to raise a subscription that would enable him perhaps to buy a house and live comfortably, he was unsuccessful. People knew, from experience, of Beethoven's awkward and contradictory behaviour. 'The very next day after he was provided with a house,' they told him, 'he'd be just as likely to sell it.'

While Beethoven struggled in his untidy room with the majestic piano sonatas which belong to his last period, Rossini attended gala dinners with the leading citizens of Vienna and appeared nightly to receive the excited applause of audiences who packed theatres to cheer him. After the last performance of the season, a crowd of enthusiastic Viennese assembled beneath his window and would not go until the troupe, who were about to have supper, had given several encores. Rossini himself obliged by singing 'Largo al factotum' from the *Barbiere*. All the time he was in Vienna, like a television personality of today he was recognized in the street and people ran up to see him pass.

At the end of their four-month stay in the city Rossini and his wife took to the road again, this time bearing with them a silver vase full of ducats given by his Viennese admirers. That summer they relaxed in Isabella's villa at Castenaso, and for a few weeks Rossini composed little music. By the last months of the year they were in Verona, where an important diplomatic congress was being held. Rossini had been invited to write a cantata for the occasion, and since, as he wryly observed, the politicians assembled there could find little to agree about, he felt obliged to help with some music 'where harmony was needed so badly'. It was here that he met the Duke of Wellington, a keen music lover who, as a boy, had delighted to play the violin. The Duke was a connoisseur of Italian opera and of Italian opera singers, and we may be sure that he found the Rossinis a diverting couple. He was among the audience when Rossini himself sang, probably, the 'Largo al factotum' which had become his party piece. A little later, the same performance won Rossini a diamond ring from the Tsar of Russia.

Early next year, in 1823, Rossini presented an ambitious opera in Venice called *Semiramide*. The heroine is Semiramis, queen of Assyria, whose tragic life, punctuated by murder and crime, supplied the materials for a dark and blood-boltered melodrama. *Semiramide* is one of the longest operas Rossini ever composed, yet it took him only thirty-odd days to finish. The overture has remained famous and contains a stately *andantino*.

Andantino, *Semiramide* overture

This is played by four horns and sounds remarkably like something by Weber. It is suitably mysterious for a solemn moment in the opera where an oath of loyalty is sworn. The public took to *Semiramide*. The impressive scenery of ancient Babylon, the appearance of a real brass band on stage, and, above all, lots of brilliant opportunities for singers to thrill audiences with their virtuosity, combined to gain Rossini new followers. What is more, the opera set the seal on his European reputation. Escorted triumphantly home by a procession of gondolas, he was not to know that *Semiramide* would be the last piece he ever wrote for the Italian stage.

London now tempted Rossini and his wife with a handsome engagement at the King's Theatre. In October 1823 they embarked on the long journey and spent some time in Paris on the way. This was Rossini's first experience of Paris, and in spite of jealousy and opposition in several quarters there, he was pleased on the whole with the reception that greeted him. Leading French composers offered him a lavish banquet. He was applauded and serenaded. Parisian society vied in giving parties for him. The visit was, in short, the warmest possible introduction to the capital.

Then came the agony of the Channel crossing. It was December and the ship rolled horribly. Never a good sailor at any time, Rossini suffered tortures of sea-sickness. For days he groaned in misery and despaired of reaching England alive. On arrival in London he collapsed into bed with a chill and stayed there for a week. His rooms were in Regent Street, and when he recovered he would sit with a pet parrot and marvel at the crowds and traffic that whirled below. At the end of the month he went to Brighton and visited the Duke of Clarence (who was to become William IV) at the gaudy Pavilion, where the exotic decorations must have reminded him of the settings of some of his operas. He sang, to his own accompaniment, several arias 'with true comic spirit and humour', reported a newspaper. The Duke was overjoyed. Several times during Rossini's London visit they performed duets together, the Duke in a rumbling bass and the composer in a crisp baritone.

With such royal favour behind him, Rossini could not help but conquer

London. He was much in demand at parties, and the 'fat, natural, jolly-looking person, with a sort of vague archness in his eye', soon became a popular social figure. Lords and ladies pursued him with high fees for the honour of his presence at their houses. Somebody gave him a large block of shares, and another patron offered him £200 (about $560) for two appearances in his drawing-room. What with the money he made from his theatre engagement and the cash that poured in from lessons and 'personal appearances', Rossini did very well indeed. All in all, he made nearly £40,000 (about $113,000) in modern currency from his stay in London. It was the largest single sum he ever earned, and it enabled him, with the aid of shrewd investment, to live in comfort for the rest of his life without any real need to work. Yet, as he pointed out, it came to him not as a direct result of his music but from the teaching, conducting and accompanying he had done. The only music he wrote in London was a piece on the death of Lord Byron—and a large part of this was taken from an opera he had written some time previously!

There was a brief visit to Cambridge, where Rossini sang not only 'Largo al factotum' but also 'God Save the King' in eccentric English, and the scene moved back to London. After renewing acquaintance with the Duke of Wellington, who threw a great party in their honour at the suggestion of George IV, the Rossinis prepared for the dreaded Channel voyage.

It was summer 1824, and this time the sea was calmer. Apart from the boredom he felt on the traditional English Sunday, Rossini departed from London with pleasant memories and full pockets. In Paris the French authorities, perhaps inspired by news of his London triumphs, offered him a well-paid post as director of the Théâtre-Italien. This theatre was second only in importance to the Paris Opéra itself, and the situation would give Rossini great influence besides assuring him control over the production of his own works. He accepted. In the large apartments which he took on the boulevard Montmartre, he and his wife entertained plentifully and confirmed the good impression made when they had passed through the town nearly a year ago. There he would get up late in the morning and exchange news, witticisms and gossip with friends who formed the habit of dropping in to see him. They could always be sure of a good meal and good conversation.

At this period, too, he began to acquire a mastery of French that surprised his new colleagues. He spoke and wrote French with a fluency and a ready use of idiom as if he had been born to it.

He was still only thirty-two years old. Quite apart from his position as a leading European composer, he now held an important official post which, for most musicians, would have been the peak of a lifetime's career. He was doubly fortunate. Naturally, there were French people who disliked the idea of a foreigner being given such a lot of power in the musical world. Always sensitive to opinion, Rossini entered on his new duties with caution. It was almost a year before he produced a new opera, and it was not one of his best. *Il viaggio a Reims* also has the odd distinction of being the longest one-act opera ever written, as it was said to have lasted for three hours. This unfortunate work quickly vanished into obscurity and Rossini was ill for several months.

On his recovery he was able to make up to a certain extent for his initia failure. The opportunity was the first French production at the Théâtre-Italien of a new opera by the young German composer Meyerbeer. Rossini supervised it with great care, and the result was a splendid success. In this way he helped to launch Meyerbeer on a career which was to make him one of the most dominating figures in French opera. Rossini's own operas during his direction of the theatre had mixed fortunes. Only *le Siège de Corinthe*, which has been mentioned earlier, roused much enthusiasm, and that was chiefly because the war of Greek independence against the Turkish overlord made the subject topical.

To add to Rossini's worries at the time, he heard from Bologna that his mother was gravely ill with heart trouble. Soon afterwards she died. One of the few things that the usually gay Rossini took seriously was his relationship with his parents. He loved them both. When people reproached him for the careless way he had written his operas and eked them out with music from his other works, he would answer: 'The time and money allowed me for composing were so small that I scarcely had time to read the libretti I had to set. All I really cared about was the support of my dearly loved parents and poor relations.' Like most Italians Rossini was devoted to his family. His mother's death, though not unexpected, was something he never really recovered from.

When, shortly afterwards, the Paris production of *Moïse* evoked the warm applause it had drawn several years before in Naples, he was still suffering from the shock. He took his curtain call on the first night in front of a cheering audience and whispered to himself: 'But she is dead!' It was a sad irony that at last, when he was beginning to consolidate his position in Paris, a deep sorrow should have spoilt the happiness he would otherwise have felt.

By now he had resigned from the Théâtre-Italien. The government made him a generous allowance and bestowed on him the grand title of 'First Composer to the King and Inspector-General of Singing in France'. Everybody knew that this royal appointment was simply an excuse to keep the famous composer in Paris. Rossini was amused. He would sometimes wander on the boulevards listening with close attention to the street singers. If asked what he was doing, he would gravely reply that he was gathering material for his official report as Inspector-General. His proud father, old Vivazza, came to stay with him. Overawed by the royal favour shown to his son, he told acquaintances in Bologna: 'Paris is a real fine place to live in, and he is real popular and has lots of friends.'

Curiously enough, Rossini composed one of his most cheerful comic operas not long after his mother's death. He may have wanted to get away from the melancholy circumstances that had dogged him lately, and he chose for the purpose an amusing old legend set in the Middle Ages. Count Ory has fallen in love with Adèle, a beautiful countess whose brother is away on the Crusades. The designing count and his followers dress themselves as nuns and get into the castle where Adèle and her ladies await the return of her brother and his soldier companions. The plot has many complicated situations, including one where a page is dressed as a woman and is mistaken by Ory for Adèle. Suddenly there is an alarming commotion: the brother is back from the Crusades and about to enter the castle! Adèle forgives Count Ory and his men their naughty trick and helps them escape just in time.

Rossini wrote *le comte Ory* while staying in the country house of a new friend, the Spanish banker Aguado. The latter was a clever financier who helped him with his investments and advised him on the use of his money. While out fishing with Aguado, Rossini once said, his feet in the water and his friend talking about Spanish finance, that he composed the overture to *le comte Ory* in his head. The overture, and indeed the whole opera, flashes along with all the brightness characteristic of Rossini in the days before he started writing tragedy to please Isabella Colbran. *Le comte Ory* is at present in the Sadler's Wells repertory, and a visit there will show you why many people believe this opera to be one of his finest. Berlioz was among the first to praise it, and he declared there was enough in it to ensure the success of several ordinary operas besides. Though it may seem to lack the spontaneous humour of the *Barbiere* or the sweet poignancy of *Cenerentola*, it certainly does not come far behind them in gracefulness, refinement and freshness of writing.

In the second act we hear what Berlioz described as 'that wonderful trio', 'à la faveur de cette nuit obscure'. It is the point at which Count Ory, Adéle and the page are embroiled, 'under cover of this dark night', in one of the plot's misunderstandings. The lovely orchestral introduction, with its gentle chromatic sighs, begins:

'A la faveur de cette nuit obscure', *Comte Ory*

It reminds us that Rossini admired Mozart above all other composers, and here he shows himself a worthy disciple.

In addition to its great merits, *le comte Ory* is a notable date for the history of French music. Before composing it, Rossini, who is so often accused of slapdash methods, had carefully appraised the French style. He had taken practical advice from singers about setting to music what was, for him, a foreign language, and had adjusted his own very Italian manner to French taste. His opera, though it was slow in gaining favour, received no less than sixty performances in the year, by which time people had realized they were hearing something that was unusually original. What happened was that Rossini had written a work destined to influence French opera and operetta for many years to come. It was no small achievement for an Italian to have altered the musical development of the country he had adopted.

Ever since that time *le comte Ory* has been the delight of connoisseurs. Liszt produced it at his theatre and described the melodies as 'flowing like champagne'. We already know how highly Berlioz thought of it. Rossini was the king of Paris and everyone acknowledged his victory. Yet even before *le comte Ory* reached its third performance, he had slipped away to the peace of the countryside to write another work that would turn out to be a masterpiece.

A French cartoonist's amusing impression of Rossini
as a 'one-man band'

VII

William Tell and the Stabat Mater

For nearly a year musical Paris buzzed with speculation about the new opera Rossini was writing. The newspapers were full of contradictory reports, and public interest was thoroughly aroused. By the time *Guillaume Tell* was announced as being ready for performance in August 1829, excitement had become intense. Yet, after such a long period of anticipation, the audience at the first night could not help feeling disappointed by the result. They were presented with a very long opera composed in a different style from what they expected of Rossini, and their reaction was not enthusiastic. Somebody even described the new opera as 'cold and boring'.

On the other hand, critics and musicians immediately recognized the true value of *Guillaume Tell*. Its main drawback—and this could not be blamed on Rossini—was the clumsy libretto. Even so, the famous story of William Tell and his brave struggle to overthrow the Austrian tyrant gave the composer many opportunities to write some of the finest music he ever produced. We have already looked at the overture and seen how charmingly it evokes the Swiss countryside, its lakes, mountains and sudden storms followed by calm. The first act opens with a chorus of high quality. To the accompaniment of a pair of harps, fishermen greet the clear sky as a promise of serene weather to come:

'Quel jour serein', *Guillaume Tell*

William Tell and the Stabat Mater

This melody is typical of the pastoral note Rossini struck with delightful simplicity throughout the whole opera. By contrast, the powerful ensemble where the Swiss defiantly shout 'Aux armes!' shows that he had lost none of his gift for exciting tunes.

Many people believe that Act II is the best part of *Guillaume Tell*, and it has been said that Wagner and Verdi can offer nothing to better this section. It contains a lively hunting fanfare, several choruses which are cleverly adapted to the characters who sing them, and various pieces of unique beauty for individual performers. Of these, the loveliest is perhaps the aria sung by the heroine Mathilde:

'Sombres forêts', *Guillaume Tell*

tur — bine im-pe — ra al – la cal-ma, al – la cal-ma il

mi – o cor s'a-pri – rà. L'e-co sol,

l'e – co sol le mie

pe — — ne, le mie

pe — ne u – di – rà, u – di .– rà.

E

Elsewhere in the opera comes the sprightly ballet music, famous on its own account and later used in part by Benjamin Britten for the popular *Soirées musicales* and *Matinées musicales*, and the moving scene when Tell shoots the apple from his son's head.

Although public approval was slow to come, *Guillaume Tell* went on being performed at the Paris Opéra and eventually won a loyal following. It was such a long work that as time passed the management began to cut large sections out of it. This caused Rossini understandable bitterness. The director of the Opéra met him one day and told him: 'We're giving Act II of *Guillaume Tell* this evening.' 'Oh,' replied the composer cynically, 'the whole of it?'

This opera, which had cost him so much effort, was the last he wrote. He certainly tried to put the best of himself into it. The reason why *Guillaume Tell* stands alone among his works is that although it inspired some great music from him, the nature of the subject was not really fitted to a man like Rossini. The story is a heroic one and Rossini was not given to heroics. What he wrote was noble and worthy, but it is not the spontaneous expression of his true character, as are his earlier comic operas. He seemed to realize this, and towards the end of his life he predicted that only the last act of *Otello*, the second act of *Tell*, and the *Barbiere*, would survive him. Still,

66

nothing to do with Rossini is ever as simple as it may seem, and *Guillaume Tell* remains a strangely inconsistent masterpiece.

Shortly after his new opera had had its first performance, Rossini and his wife Isabella went back to Italy for a time. During this period he loafed about and spent the days in gossip with Bolognese friends. Then he toyed with the idea of setting Goethe's *Faust* as an opera. Nothing came of this and so the field was left open to Gounod. In the meantime there was a political revolution in Paris. King Charles X, with whom Rossini had signed his contract, had been forced to abdicate. He was succeeded by King Louis-Philippe who had little time for music and did not wish to continue the lucrative arrangement by which Rossini enjoyed a handsome allowance from the royal court. Only after years of long and tedious lawsuits was Rossini able to lay hands on the money due to him. In the complicated negotiations that followed he was helped by his banker friend Aguado, whose skilled business brain was on many occasions to be a valuable aid.

When Rossini next visited Paris he left Isabella in Italy. They were not on the best of terms by now. She had reached the age of forty-five aware that both her voice and her beauty were vanishing fast. Accustomed to the applause of opera audiences, she found it difficult to put up with a life of monotonous calm. Her boredom led her on a frenzied search for distraction, and she ended up a heavy gambler. Annoyed by her extravagance, Rossini put her under the watchful eye of his father. Old Vivazza did what he could to keep her in order. He was just as stubborn a character as she was, and the household in Bologna was enlivened by many a storm over Isabella's expensive habits. Her temper was not improved when she reflected on the difference between her own situation, that of a fading and forgotten opera star, and that of her husband, still a young man and fêted wherever he went.

Meanwhile Rossini stayed on longer than he had intended in Paris. The arguments over his contract embroiled him in many legal battles, and the affair dragged on interminably. To take his mind off these tiresome matters, he went on holiday with Aguado to Spain, where the King, as a mark of the highest favour, offered him his half-smoked cigar ('I don't smoke,' was Rossini's diplomatic reply), and the music lovers of Madrid serenaded him beneath his window. Back in Paris a cholera epidemic drove him away once again, and the kindly Aguado family took him to relax in the south of France. Round about this time he became very ill. His wife, sulking in Bologna, was unable to help. Fortunately there was someone at hand, who was ready, anxious even, to nurse him, and in Olympe Pélissier he found the companion he wanted.

William Tell and the Stabat Mater

Olympe Pélissier was in her early thirties when she first met Rossini. She was no great beauty. Once her youth had passed, someone said, what you noticed most about her was her big Roman nose and the flashy diamonds she liked to wear. She made up for her lack of physical attraction by her intelligence. Born in poor and obscure circumstances, she rose to become the companion of famous artists and influential men. Her marriage to a wealthy but aged financier, who conveniently died soon afterwards, left her with a handsome fortune of her own. Rossini took to her immediately. Her past caused him no jealousy and he turned a blind eye to it for the sake of her amusing and outspoken conversation, her cheerfulness and the kindness with which she looked after him. She was the complete opposite of the feckless Isabella. A good organiser, careful with money and fierce as a tiger in defending Rossini's interests, she protected him from anything likely to upset him. For close on forty years she was to be an influence for good in his life.

There is no doubt that Rossini was in a bad way at this period. His nerves were in such a state that the slightest incident was enough to plunge him into a black mood. He also suffered from syphilis which caused him much pain and fatigue. Olympe nursed him through it all with devotion. Despite his ailments he managed to compose the *Soirées musicales*, a set of twelve arias and duets written with the lightest and most elegant touch. This does not mean that they are trivial. Although they may be classed as miniatures, they are miniatures of accomplished artistry. The tarantella for soprano was later to be used in the ballet *la Boutique fantasque* which Respighi, the twentieth-century Italian composer, put together out of Rossini's music. Wagner transcribed one of the pieces for orchestra and Liszt arranged them for piano. Neither of these musicians would have taken such care over trifles.

Under Olympe's attentive protection Rossini was soon well enough to tour Germany with the Rothschild family. In Frankfurt he made the acquaintance of Mendelssohn, who, despite an early unfavourable impression, told his sister of Rossini's '. . . intelligence, vivacity, and polish at all times and in every word; and whoever doesn't think him a genius must hear him hold forth only once, and he'll change his mind immediately'. Rossini, for his part, enjoyed Mendelssohn's playing of Bach, though he could not understand why such an obviously talented musician did not write operas.

When at last Rossini's affairs in Paris were straightened out, he decided to settle in Bologna. The problem of Isabella, to whom the exasperated

Vivazza now referred satirically as 'My lady, the Duchess of Castenaso', was solved by drawing up a legal separation. Isabella agreed to this, as obviously they could not carry on together. Olympe moved herself and her belongings to Bologna, where, to observe the proprieties, she installed herself at a different address from Rossini. It was not the complete answer, but the arrangement was the best they could make under the circumstances.

At the time of his separation from Isabella in 1837, Rossini was forty-five years old. It is probable that he had already taken the decision which, as soon as it became known, was to astonish his public and to puzzle musical scholars for generations. His resolve, quite simply, was to retire and write no more operas. Many explanations have been offered for this abrupt withdrawal from a brilliantly successful career which had made him an international figure idolized throughout Europe. The most obvious is that he was exhausted by the strain of having written nearly forty operas in twenty years, sometimes at the rate of three or four in a year. Any sort of creative effort is tiring, and the energy needed to write a book, a play, or an opera can make a heavy drain on a man's resources. Rossini's work, moreover, had been done in the hectic atmosphere of the theatre. He had had to bear with the demands of impresarios and the antics of singers. There had been, above all, the fear of any creative artist who lives by the theatre, that of failing to please the public. It is no wonder that all these things combined to destroy the health of one whose nerves were as delicate as Rossini's. Besides, he was now a rich man and there was no need for him to continue an existence which, though it had brought him fame and money, had also brought him much worry and sickness.

Other events helped to sap Rossini's vitality. In 1839 Vivazza died at the age of eighty. The death of his last surviving parent threw him into a collapse. 'I have lost everything most precious that I have on earth . . .' he wrote to a friend. The prospect of travelling anywhere filled him with dread, and a train journey actually made him faint. He hardly slept at all and even lost his taste for food. The famous dish, *tournedos Rossini*, which had been named after him and which still appears on menus today, failed to please him. He no longer enjoyed the ripe Bolognese cheeses and hams that he had once attacked with such relish. Only the devoted nursing of Olympe saved him from an early death. In search of convalescence they went to Naples, the scene of his youthful triumphs, where his old friend Barbaja lent them a villa. Still he could not recover from his mood of listlessness. His physical state grew worse and he went on losing weight.

In Bologna Rossini was made consultant to the Liceo Musicale, the school where he had received his own musical training. Illness had caused him to drop the mask of cynicism and carelessness which he usually wore, and friends were impressed by the conscientious way he tackled his rather boring duties. Another unexpected side to his character was revealed by his treatment of the young opera composer Bellini. We have already seen how generous Rossini was in acknowledging his junior's talent. He followed Bellini's career with encouraging interest, and after the composer's death at the tragically early age of thirty-three, it was Rossini who cleared up his estate. He also made himself helpful to Meyerbeer and Donizetti, both of them potential rivals in the field of opera. These are not the actions of a man who could be described as frivolous and selfish.

Neither is it fair to say Rossini was lazy. Although he had given up writing operas, he went on composing music, large quantities of it, until the end of his life. In 1839 he decided to complete a setting of the *Stabat Mater* which he had begun a few years earlier. A music firm had acquired rights to the six numbers already written and intended to publish them. Spurred into action, Rossini hastened to finish the last four numbers and gave the rights to his own publisher. The text of the *Stabat Mater* has been set by other composers—Palestrina, Haydn, Schubert, Liszt, Verdi and Dvorák among them—and is part of the mass sung in Catholic churches on certain days of the year. The Latin words were written in the thirteenth century and depict the sorrow of Mary at the sufferings of Jesus. The title comes from the opening verse, '*Stabat Mater dolorosa/Juxta crucem lacrymosa . . .*' meaning: 'Sadly the mother stood/Weeping near the Cross.'

If you are accustomed to the austere religious music of Bach, you may at first think Rossini's a little light-hearted by contrast. The best-known item in the *Stabat Mater* is a springy tenor aria, '*Cujus animam gementem*' ('Her sorrowing heart'), which sounds more like the sort of plaint an operatic hero would address to his lover than a lament for Christ's mother. Yet there is nothing irreverent about it. When people reproached Haydn for the apparent lack of gravity in his oratorios, he replied that he could not help being joyful at the thought of God. It was the same with Rossini. He could not hide his true feelings with a sham seriousness which was foreign to his nature. He wrote with a sincere Italian exuberance and poured into the *Stabat Mater* all the warmth and humanity which his religion inspired in him.

What is more, Rossini brought to this work the very special tenderness which he cherished for his own mother. You have only to hear the unaccompanied chorus '*Quando corpus morietur*' ('When my body perishes') to realize the magnificent quality of the writing:

'Quando corpus morietur', *Stabat Mater*

The *Stabat* was first given in Paris in 1842 and was warmly received. A few months later a performance in Bologna was equally successful. Rossini's fellow-townsmen gathered in the street and cheered him when he appeared on a balcony to thank them. But after the final rehearsal, it is said, he rushed off to be on his own. He looked at a picture of his mother and wept. Once again he felt a stinging sadness that she could not be there to join in his success.

The *Stabat* left Rossini in a very emotional state. About this time the death of his friend Aguado, whose kindness and advice he had prized, increased his depression. The pain of syphilis and other physical complications was now so bad that a course of treatment by a leading Paris surgeon became necessary. The cure was long and slow, but he returned to Bologna feeling much better. For the next few years he wrote hardly any music. An opera put on in Paris and called *Robert Bruce* was a hotch-potch clumsily assembled from his earlier works. Berlioz attacked it sharply. The faithful Olympe, purple with rage at his disrespectful remarks, made sure Berlioz knew what she thought of him by wrapping up a pair of donkey's ears in a parcel and sending them to him.

Grave news arrived in the summer of 1845. Isabella Colbran was seriously ill. Her husband had had little to do with her for eight years or so, but he went over to Castenaso to see her. They were alone in her sickroom for half an hour, at the end of which he came out with tears gushing down his cheeks. Their reunion brought back memories that were painful to him. Nearly thirty years ago Isabella had been queen of the Neapolitan stage. Rossini had been gay with all the carelessness of youth, and their collaboration then had been a sparkling partnership between his lively genius and her surpassing beauty. Now she was a raddled sixty-year-old on her deathbed and he a broken, prematurely aged man of fifty-three. Despite her tiresome character and her wayward habits, she had loved him. A few weeks later she died, still speaking his name.

Rossini never went back to her villa at Castenaso. It was sold as soon as possible after her death. At last he was able to marry Olympe Pélissier. The ceremony took place one summer's day in 1846, and Olympe's long-delayed reward for all her faithful service came with the right to call herself Signora Rossini, a right she was to enjoy with pride for over thirty years.

Music written by Rossini in a friend's autograph album

VIII

A 'Sinful' Old Age

Life is not always such an easy, cut-and-dried matter as events may sometimes suggest. Though Rossini had waited for a long time before he could marry Olympe, when the opportunity finally came it was clouded by his genuine mourning for the unhappy Isabella. No sooner, moreover, had he settled down to his new way of existence than political events began to threaten his peace of mind. The year 1848 was a time of revolutions throughout Europe. The unrest spread to Bologna, and a local politician organized a hostile demonstration outside Rossini's house because the composer was thought to be lukewarm in his attitude to the new 'liberal' ideas. Rossini was not the slightest bit interested in politics. He had not inherited his father's passion for political argument, and all he wanted was a quiet life.

Thoroughly unnerved by the distressing experience of seeing people booing him outside his own home, he packed his belongings and left Bologna the very next morning. Olympe fully agreed with his decision and was angry at the small group of Bolognese who had upset her beloved. He was never to live there again, despite pleas from the townsmen to return. Instead, the Rossinis made their headquarters in the lovely old town of Florence, where local society gave him a welcome that helped to make up for the Bologna setback. The two of them lived there quietly for a while in the company of 'a moth-eaten, nauseating, pestilential dog', which, though it annoyed their guests, received from Olympe almost as much adoration as she gave to her husband.

Rossini needed all the attention she could lavish on him, for he had sunk into a deplorable condition. Even Olympe failed to reawaken his interest in music. He would break into sudden fits of sobbing for no reason at all. Over a long period he was dogged by sleeplessness and could only doze off for five minutes at a time. His face grew withered and his eyes listless. Food left him indifferent. He thought of killing himself—but '. . . I am a

Pen-and-ink sketch by Rossini on the back of an envelope showing
himself (right) and a friend during his stay in Florence

coward and haven't the courage to do it.' The rumour spread that he had
gone mad.

He took cures at various health resorts, but still to no avail. He remained
unable to dress or undress himself without help. Worse, whenever he heard
music, the sound of the major third reverberated in his head. In the end
Olympe took a desperate step. She persuaded him that a stay in Paris and
a change of scenery might serve to restore him. After a lengthy and tiring
journey they arrived in the capital and were greeted with the old excitement
and pleasure his name had always inspired there. His French doctors put
him on a strict régime and throughout the summer of 1855, ever so gradually, he began to improve. Visits to the seaside and tours of German spas
helped him forward. By July he was feeling well enough to talk about music
—something he had not done for months.

In the autumn of 1855 the Rossinis took a spacious flat in Paris on the
corner of the rue de la Chaussée d'Antin and the boulevard des Italiens. It
was, and remains today, a busy intersection of two main thoroughfares.

A 'Sinful' Old Age

When, as often happened, Rossini could not sleep, he amused himself by watching the crowds who strolled along below. The sun streamed into his bedroom through large windows and lit up a bed arched with a canopy and curtains. Over the years this room became filled with knick-knacks of every sort—a clock surmounted with a bust of Mozart, signed photographs of kings and queens, copies of famous paintings, and a massive cupboard where Rossini stored his manuscripts. In this room, at a little upright piano, he tried out new compositions. Next door was a smaller room, even more tightly crammed with oddities which included a Scottish tobacco jar, old musical instruments and ancient weapons. The rest of the apartment consisted of Olympe's bedroom and boudoir, a reception hall, an ample drawing-room, and a dining-room, with, needless to say, a substantial kitchen.

Each morning Rossini was up at eight o'clock and taking a modest breakfast. After receiving visitors he would put on his big hat, stick a pin bearing a medallion of Handel into his cravat, and take the air on the boulevards. He soon became known and respected at the local grocer's where he bought food for the household. The grocer once tried to pass off Genoese macaroni as being Neapolitan. Rossini was not deceived and astonished the tradesman with his expert knowledge. Someone then told the grocer who Rossini was.

'Rossini?' said the grocer. 'I don't know him. But if he's as well up in music as he is in macaroni, then he must write some lovely stuff!'

At six o'clock Rossini had his dinner and smoked a cigar. He usually went early to bed. On Saturday evenings he stayed up late and gave dinner parties. These Saturday evenings were famous social occasions, and people vied eagerly for an invitation. At one time or another most of the great names of Paris found their way to Number 2 rue de la Chaussée d'Antin. At Rossini's piano, Liszt gave the first performance of his *Saint François de Paule marchant sur les flots*. Verdi was present in the drawing-room to hear the quartet from his opera *Rigoletto*. Gounod and Meyerbeer were often to be seen there, together with the young virtuoso Saint-Saëns, whom Rossini had taken under his wing, and practically every composer, player and singer who had any claim to distinction. Fashionable women and their escorts crowded so thickly into the drawing-room that anyone who wished to play the piano had literally to fight his way through.

Rossini himself preferred to sit quietly with a few close friends in the dining-room, where he left the door open for whoever wished to talk to him. He was now very bald, and each Saturday he would carefully select a wig from his large selection to conceal the shiny dome about which he was rather sensitive. His wit remained as sharp as ever. 'Oh, I was so fright-

ened!' confessed a lady who had just sung an aria with great amateurish-
ness. 'So was I, Madame,' said Rossini blandly. A famous tenor, noted for
a top C♯ which sent his hearers into raptures, was announced one evening.
'Show him in,' answered Rossini, 'but tell him to leave his C♯ with the hats
and coats outside. He can take it with him when he goes.'

Manuscript written in 1858. A canon for four sopranos—perhaps one of the
'Sins of my old age'

The highlight of these evenings came when the host decided to play some
of his own music. Guests fell back respectfully as Rossini waddled up to the
piano and seated his squat bulk on the stool. 'I'm only a simple fourth-class
pianist,' he warned with mock-modesty. He was nothing of the sort, of
course, but instead was a very fine performer. He rarely used the pedals,
and his fingers, though small and plump, danced over the keyboard with
astonishing lightness. The pieces he played were usually items from the
hundreds he composed during the last dozen years of his life and which he
called *Péchés de vieillesse* ('Sins of my old age'). His return to composition
was marked in 1857 by a little suite he gave to Olympe for her birthday
entitled *Musique anodine* ('Soothing music'). From then onwards he wrote
music with the speed and facility for which he had been noted in his youth.
Some of his pieces he called *Riens* ('Trifles'), and among them was this pen-
sive melody which is familiar to ballet audiences:

Andantino mosso, *Quelques riens pour album*

Only a small number of Rossini's 'sins' have been published. Even during his lifetime it was not easy to obtain a hearing of them, for Olympe jealously locked them away as soon as they were written and would only release them by special request. They include miniatures for piano, songs, duets, and chamber music for different combinations of instruments. The titles are deliberately quaint or grotesque, and they foreshadow the custom of the modern French musician Erik Satie, who also liked to give his pieces odd names. There are, for example, a 'Hygienic prelude for morning use', a 'Convulsive prelude' and a 'So-called dramatic prelude'. For dancing there are a 'Limping waltz', 'Miscarriage of a polka mazurka', and a 'Thorough-bred tarantella'. A touch of romance is provided by 'Love in Peking' (a little song on the Chinese scale), and old friends are not forgotten in 'A word to Paganini'. Another suite called *Four hors d'oeuvres* is made up of 'Radishes', with themes and variations on anchovies, gherkins and butter. Players of the 'Fanfare for four hands' are asked to perform 'my little fanfare with love' and, in a sly addition, 'with hands and knees'. A quirky series of 'comico-imitative' numbers depicts a pleasure trip by train which ends in a 'terrible derailment' after the 'sweet melody of the brake' and 'devilish whistling'. 'You won't catch me in it,' adds Rossini, who was terrified of the new-fangled railway. Yet however comic the title of these 'sins', the music is always elegantly harmonized and full of neat ideas which continually bubble forth to surprise and delight the listener.

And so the years passed by in music making and sociable evenings. Parisian summers were inclined to be too stuffy for Rossini, and he bought some land at Passy, a suburb noted for its rural beauty. He chose the plot, according to rumour, because it was shaped like a grand piano. Garbed in a floppy overcoat and nankeen trousers, he ceremoniously laid the first stone and Olympe planted a rose tree. Around the light and airy villa that was built on the site bloomed flowerbeds in the shape of various musical instruments. Another amusing idea was the gilt lyre, which, when hoisted up on the main gate, indicated to passers-by that the musically-minded owner was in residence.

In the spring of 1860, while preparing his opera *Tannhäuser* for its Paris production, Richard Wagner came to pay a courtesy call on Rossini. It was an odd meeting. At first the two men treated each other with respectful, if guarded, curiosity. Wagner had heard accounts of Rossini's witticisms at the expense of his music which were less than kind. Rossini, on the other hand, was not unaware that Wagner had written spitefully about him. Yet despite the vast differences between the arrogant German and the genial, disillusioned Italian, they were soon on very good terms. A long and amiable discussion followed, and Rossini was broadminded enough to accept many of the new ideas Wagner hoped to introduce into opera. Although, in Wagner's eyes, he represented the old school of opera, Rossini was far too intelligent not to appreciate the need for reform. In fact, as Wagner pointed out to him, Rossini himself had anticipated the 'new' music in his own *Guillaume Tell*. 'So,' commented Rossini impishly, 'I was writing music of the future without realizing it?'

They talked on into the afternoon, these two composers who, in spite of being completely unlike in their characters and their work, had a common devotion to an art which they both served with genius. The encounter which gossips had forecast would end in violent quarrels was, on the contrary, an enlightened occasion. They agreed on their admiration for Weber and Beethoven. Rossini told how he trained himself in the early years by writing orchestral accompaniments to the vocal lines of Haydn and Mozart, and then learned from his mistakes by comparing his own version with the originals. But when Wagner praised some of Rossini's works he interrupted: 'What is it all worth when compared with the work of a Mozart or a Haydn?' Mozart, he repeated, was 'the angel of music'. For Wagner, Rossini was ever afterwards 'the only true great' musician he met in Paris. As he was taking his leave, Rossini showed him a mechanical organ that stood in the dining-room. It started to play popular old Italian songs, and Rossini said: 'Who's the unknown composer? Some village fiddler, apparently. These songs probably date from far back, yet they live still. Will there remain as much of *us* a century from now?'

Bach, Rossini had told Wagner, was a miracle of God. Rossini had come late to Bach, and it was only during his old age that he fully appreciated him. Bach's influence on Rossini may be seen in the last important work he wrote. This he called the *Petite messe solennelle*, and it is typical of his humour that, as a mass, it is neither small nor particularly solemn. He worked at it through the summer of 1863, and it seems to have given him quite a lot of trouble. 'Dear God,' he wrote, 'here is this poor little Mass, finished at last. Have I written truly sacred music or just damned bad music? Thou knowest I was born for comic opera! Not much skill but quite a bit of feeling—that's how I'd sum it up. Blessed be Thy name, and grant me Paradise.'

These words, coming from a man such as Rossini, contain no disrespect. They are, rather, a mark of his sincerity, for although he believed deeply in God he certainly did not believe in pompousness. This attitude sets the mood of his 'little' mass. Like the *Stabat Mater*, it is a mixture of happy rejoicing in God and of reflective tenderness. The operatic Rossini is represented by a jolly tenor solo, 'Domine Deus', which is a counterpart of the 'Cujus animam' in the *Stabat Mater*. Equally virile, but still more moving in its vibrant solemnity, is the second part of the 'Et resurrexit' ('And he shall rise again on the third day'):

'Et resurrexit', *Petite messe solennelle*

The mass was originally intended for a modest accompaniment of two pianos and harmonium. Afraid that other hands might tamper with it when he was gone, Rossini later orchestrated it. The *Petite messe solennelle* was given several times in private and much impressed the musicians who heard it. It was never played in public while Rossini was alive, and even after his death it did not receive many performances. Only today, thanks to a fine new recording and to the general reawakening of interest in Rossini, are people beginning to acknowledge its beauty. There are moments, it is true, when the music shines with the glitter of the theatre and when the footlights do not seem far away. What is most striking about the work is the heartfelt emotion which gives it such conviction. The part-writing is beautifully dovetailed and the fugue is an exciting masterpiece of construction.

Apart from the *Hymne à Napoléon III*, an 'official' piece written for the 1867 Exhibition, and including a cannon among the large forces specified in the score—'Forgive such meagreness!' joked Rossini—there was little more to come from the pen of the musician whom his admirers had dubbed 'the Swan of Pesaro'. He lingered on long enough into 1868 to celebrate one of his rare birthdays, his seventy-sixth according to the calendar, but only his eighteenth if leap years are taken into account. For once he did not enjoy the joke. He knew he was desperately ill, and the celebrations organized in his honour failed to console him for the knowledge that soon he was to leave the bright world he loved so much.

Towards the end of the year Rossini underwent a painful operation. It left him very weak. He sank into delirium and muttered pathetic appeals to the Virgin Mary and to his mother. Late one night he spoke his wife's name: 'Olympe'. It was, appropriately for a superstitious man, the ominous date of the 13th November. Then he died. 'Rossini,' cried Olympe, throwing herself on the body, 'I shall always be worthy of you.' And so she was until her own death ten years later, a period during which she defended her husband's memory with the same fierce loyalty she had shown him in his lifetime.

Rossini died at the end of a career which is unique in the history of music. His character and his music, full of contradictions and unexpected turns, have never ceased to fascinate people ever since. Over four thousand mourners crowded into the church for his funeral. Among the music they heard was the 'Quis est homo?' ('Who is the man that does not weep at seeing Christ's mother in such affliction?') from the *Stabat Mater*. It was sung 'as it never had been before' by two of the most famous sopranos of the time, Marietta Alboni and Adelina Patti:

'Quis est homo?' *Stabat Mater*

This should be enough to show us that Rossini was much more than just a writer of comic opera. He was not only the creator of Figaro's wit, the glitter of Cinderella and the polished high spirits of Count Ory. With William Tell and his religious works, the lovingly matured inspiration of old age, he became a musician worthy of being classed among the greatest.

G. Rossini

Suggestions for Further Reading

Most of the books about Rossini are in Italian or French. An important one, by Giuseppe Radiciotti, is entitled *Gioacchino Rossini* (3 vols., 1927–9). The latest, though not the most readable, book to appear in England is Herbert Weinstock's *Rossini* (Oxford University Press, 1968). Still the best books in English are Francis Toye's *Rossini* (Arthur Barker, 1934), and Lord Derwent's amusing *Rossini and Some Forgotten Nightingales* (Duckworth, 1934), both of which capture the true spirit of the composer and are delightful to read. You can probably get them from your local library, as both are unfortunately out of print.

But it is the music that matters. The best place to appreciate Rossini is in the theatre, where he is meant to be heard. (At present Sadler's Wells regularly perform, in English translation, *The Barber of Seville*, *Cinderella*, *The Thieving Magpie* and *Count Ory*.) More of his music is now available on gramophone records, including some of the non-operatic material. Apart from the scores of his operas, which are easily obtainable, the following piano music has been published:

La Boutique fantasque (arrangement of the ballet), J. &. W. Chester, London, 1919.

Quelques riens pour piano (ed. Luigi Rognoni), Edizioni Suvini Zerboni, Milan, 1951.

5 piano pieces (ed. Soulima Stravinsky), C. F. Peters, New York, 1962.

Une Réjouissance, Faber Music, London, 1966.

A Summary of Rossini's Works

Operas

Demetrio e Polibio. Opera seria, 2 acts (Rome, 1812)

La Cambiale di matrimonio. Farsa, 1 act (Venice, 1810)

L'Equivoco stravagante. Opera buffa, 2 acts (Bologna, 1811)

L'Inganno felice. Farsa, 1 act (Venice, 1812)

Ciro in Babilonia. Dramma, 2 acts (Ferrara, 1812)

La Scala di seta. Farsa, 1 act (Venice, 1812)

La Pietra di paragone. Melodramma giocoso (Milan, 1812)

L'Occasione fa il ladro. Burletta per musica, 1 act (Venice, 1812)

Il Signor Bruschino. Farsa giocosa, 1 act (Venice, 1813)

Tancredi. Opera seria, 2 acts (Venice, 1813)

L'Italiana in Algeri. Melodramma giocoso, 2 acts (Venice, 1813)

Aureliano in Palmira. Opera seria, 2 acts (Milan, 1813)

Il Turco in Italia. Opera buffa, 2 acts (Milan, 1814)

Sigismondo. Opera seria, 2 acts (Venice, 1814)

Elisabetta, regina d'Inghilterra. Dramma, 2 acts (Naples, 1815)

Torvaldo e Dorliska. Dramma semiseria, 2 acts (Rome, 1815)

Il Barbiere di Siviglia. Opera buffa, 2 acts (Rome, 1816)

La Gazzetta. Dramma, 2 acts (Naples, 1816)

Otello. Opera seria, 3 acts (Naples, 1816)

La Cenerentola. Dramma giocosa, 2 acts (Rome, 1817)

La Gazza ladra. Melodramma, 2 acts (Milan, 1817)

Armida. Opera seria, 3 acts (Naples, 1817)

Adelaide di Borgogna. Dramma, 2 acts (Rome, 1817)

Mosè in Egitto. Azione tragico-sacra, 3 acts (Naples, 1818)

Adina. Farsa, 1 act (Lisbon, 1826)

Ricciardo e Zoraide. Dramma, 2 acts (Naples, 1818)

Ermione. Azione tragica, 2 acts (Naples, 1819)

Eduardo e Cristina. Dramma, 2 acts (Venice, 1819)

A Summary of Rossini's Works

La donna del lago. Melodramma, 2 acts (Naples, 1819)
Bianca e Falliero. Opera seria, 2 acts (Milan, 1819)
Maometta II. Dramma, 2 acts (Naples, 1820)
Matilde di Shabran. Melodramma giocoso, 2 acts (Rome, 1821)
Zelmira. Dramma, 2 acts (Naples, 1822)
Semiramide. Melodramma tragico, 2 acts (Venice, 1823)
Il viaggio a Reims. Cantata scenica, 2 acts (Paris, 1825)
Le Siège de Corinthe. Grand opera, 3 acts. (Paris, 1826)
Moïse et Pharaon. Grand opera, 4 acts (Paris, 1827)
Le Comte Ory. Opéra-comique, 2 acts (Paris, 1828)
Guillaume Tell. Grand opera, 4 acts (Paris, 1829)

(Also a number of miscellaneous entertainments for the stage made up of music written for original operas and adapted for different plots.)

Religious Works

Messa Solenne (Naples, 1820)
Stabat Mater (Paris, 1842)
La foi, l'espérance, la charité (Paris, 1824)
Petite messe solennelle (Paris, 1864)
Various settings of sacred texts.

Choral Works

Numerous cantatas and hymns, including:
Il Pianto delle muse in morte di lord Byron (London, 1824)
Hymne à Napoléon III (Paris, 1867)

Vocal and Instrumental

Many songs for solos, duet, trio, etc.
Sonate a quattro (1804)
Soirées musicales (published in Paris, 1835)
Péchés de vieillesse. Nearly 200 songs, pieces for various different instruments or ensembles, chamber music, pieces for small orchestra, etc., many of them still unpublished. Most were written in Rossini's later years.

Orchestral Works

Sinfonia di Bologna, D major (1808)
Variations in C for Clarinet and orchestra (1809)

Index

Index